MW00627401

DIY DOG FOOD

ANGELA GERTINO

DIY DOG FOOD

ANGELA GERTINO

Make Fresh and Healthy Dog
Food at Home

Copyright © 2021 Angela Gertino

All rights reserved

No part of this book may be reproduced, or transmitted in any form
or by any means, electronic, mechanical, photocopying, recording,
or otherwise, without express written permission from the author.

The information contained in this book is for personal use only and
is not allowed or intended for commercial/business use of any kind
whatsoever.

ISBN-13: 978-1-63972-702-5
ISBN-13: 978-1-63972-703-2 (ebook)
Cover design by: Angela Gertino
Photography on pages 5 and 66 by Dawn McBride of Fuzzy Love
Photography. All other photography by Angela Gertino.
Manufactured in the United States of America

CONTENTS

INTRODUCTION

Thank you for choosing to take your furbaby's nutritional health into your own hands. You'll find that with time and practice, cooking healthy meals for your dogs will become as easy as cooking for yourself. What's better is that they'll soon learn what you're doing, and it will become an event they'll want to be a part of. Just remember not to be too hard on yourself. If you've got finicky eaters, finding the right blend can be challenging, but it can also be fun. So be patient, be persistent, and you'll find success.

The recipes provided can be used for both puppies and adult dogs. If you ever have concerns or questions regarding your dog's dietary needs, it's always a good idea to discuss things with a board-certified veterinary nutritionist or your veterinarian.

If you need further help with creating recipes, or if you have a pet with special dietary needs, please visit www.mindfulmutt.com where you can schedule a private consultation to get the help you need. Here you can subscribe to the Mindful Mutt mailing list so you'll be sure to get helpful tips and important updates. You can also find Angela and her furry companions on social media @mindful.mutt where she posts all kinds of helpful content to accompany the book.

First, let's take a look at dogs and what they eat. Determining what to feed your canine family member can be one of the most important decisions you make that will greatly impact their overall health. Dogs are scavenging carnivores. Ok, well what does that mean? Dogs have adapted to living on pretty much anything they can get their paws on, and I mean literally. From meat, to veggies, fruit, garbage, you name it. The problem is that some food isn't good for them at all, while other foods will provide the nutrition they need, so that they can thrive and live long and healthful lives.

In this recipe guide, you'll learn how to create variety by choosing ingredients from different food groups. Then you'll learn how to weigh, prepare, cook, and process them to create a healthy food that your canine furbabies will love. Keep in mind that the recipe variations are limitless. I've included many example ingredients from each of the food groups to choose from; however, there are many more ingredient options from those food groups that I'm sure I didn't think of. When choosing ingredients outside of the examples in this guide, just make sure that you stick within the food groups and their weights, and of course, that they're safe for your pup. A great resource to check for dangerous plants/ingredients is aspca.org/pet-care.

DISCLAIMER

This book and any of the information it contains is never meant to replace the advice of your veterinarian, nor should it ever be used to treat, diagnose, or cure any kind of illness. If your dog is having health problems, take him/her to see a veterinarian right away. If your dog has special dietary needs, this book may not work for your dog's specific needs and should be discussed with your veterinarian or veterinary nutritionist before use. All efforts have been made to assure the accuracy of the information contained in this book as of the date of publication. The author disclaims liability for any health related outcomes that may occur as a result of applying the dietary methods suggested in this book. In no event shall the author of this book be liable for any special, consequential, incidental, or indirect damages whatsoever.

Dedicated to all the dog moms and dads out there who want to make sure their furbabies are fed nothing but the best. Thank you for being such great caretakers to your furry companions.

Also dedicated to all of the furry companions in my life, both past and present. Thank you for making me a better human being, and for showing me what unconditional love is all about.

TOOLS

WHAT YOU WILL NEED

First, let's take a look at what you'll need to get started.

• Kitchen Scale - This is by far the most important piece of equipment you'll need. If you already have one, you'll just want to make sure that it weighs in grams, ounces, and pounds. You'll also want to be sure you clearly understand how your scale works. For example, if your scale weighs in pounds, you'll want to determine if it weighs purely in pounds (1.5 lbs = 1½ lbs), or if it weighs in pounds and ounces (1 pound 8 ounces = 1½ lbs). There's an easy way to determine this if the scale doesn't display in a fairly obvious manner. Then the question becomes does the scale change at .99 or .15 - meaning, does it change from .99 to 1.0 or from .15 to 1.0? This is very important because if your scale changes at .15 to 1.0 that means that it changes in ounces. Since 16 ounces equals a pound, .8 would be a half pound instead of .5.

• Slow Cooker - I personally prefer one of the extra-large 22qt cookers because it allows me to fit a whole chicken and lots of other ingredients without overcrowding and has less risk of overflow. *Smaller cookers may need to cut the recipe in half.* You could also easily convert any boneless/ground meat recipe to the stovetop using a large stockpot. Just chop up all of your ingredients, and cook it up like you would a big batch of chili. Then stir in all of the raw and powdered ingredients (such as the fruit, any raw veggies, carbs that are cooked separately, EFA, and calcium) at the very end when you remove the pot from the heat. Then just follow the cooling and packaging instructions, and this is an easy way to make up a quick batch of food. *If using the stovetop method, you'll probably want to cut the recipe in half, unless you've got an extra large stock pot.*

•Food/Meat Thermometer – This will help ensure you've reached a safe cooking temperature and will also help ensure you're cooling the food safely prior to packaging for storage.

•"MAIN BOWL" Large mixing bowl - Trust me when I say, "The bigger the better!"

•"WEIGHT BOWL" Large transfer bowl used to get final weight of food batch before adding calcium. Since the sample recipes yield approx. 10 pounds of food, you don't absolutely need to weigh the food at the end (with the exception for puppies discussed on page 38). However, you do want to make sure that you're coming in close. It's ok to be over weight by a pound or two, especially if you add extra organ meat or eggs (discussed later), because the calcium calculation is enough calcium to cover some excess food weight based on calories. You may want to weigh your first couple batches to make sure you're getting close, and adjust accordingly.

•Large mixing spoon

•1-2 large strong slotted serving spoons or large spider skimmer (if you'll be using whole birds, like whole chicken, two comes in handy if you don't have a spider skimmer, because it allows you to put one spoon on each side of the bird to pull it out of the cooker without the bird falling apart)

•Freezer safe containers or freezer bags for packaging and storage

These are some of the main tools I have in my kitchen, but don't beat yourself up or spend a fortune if you don't already have all of them. Get creative with what you already have. As a matter of fact, some of my biggest mistakes are how I learned new ways of doing things!

INGREDIENTS

Recommended Ingredients for a Balanced Recipe

Next, let's take a look at the types of ingredients to choose and how much of them you'll need.

- Muscle Meat

- Veggies

- Carbohydrate

- Organ Meat

- Fruit

- Essential Fatty Acid (EFA)

- Calcium

- Salt (provides trace amounts of sodium and is only needed for puppies - adults are optional)

Choosing the proper ratios of whole food ingredients will allow you to easily create a healthy balanced batch of food that doesn't need to be supplemented with extra vitamins, which by the way, are usually synthetic, and are commonly from China. Whole food nutrients are so much better for your pup because they were made as nature intended.

Next we'll discuss how much of each ingredient is needed.

Ok, this is great, but how do I calculate?

Here are the ingredients and weights that you will need to make approximately 10 pounds of finished food:

- 8 pounds of meat which will cook down to about 6 pounds finished weight (this can be boneless or bone-in and then deboned after the cooking process. If you opt for bone-in, you'll want approximately 9 pounds to account for the lost bone weight)

- 2 pounds of veggies

- 1 pound of carbohydrate

- ½ pound organ meat

- ½ pound of fruit

- Essential Fatty Acid (EFA)

    - Fish source: 1 ounce per pound of meat

    - Plant based source: ¼ cup for ground seeds, or 3 tablespoons for oils

    - Calcium (we'll talk more about how much you'll need later on)

    - 2 teaspoons of salt (I prefer Himalayan)

IMPORTANT SAFETY NOTE Never give your dog cooked bones. It can end in an emergency situation or even death. We will be deboning the meat after the cooking process and the bones will be discarded. If whole raw fish is used, those bones will be crumbled into small enough pieces to be safely consumed.

PROTEINS

CHOOSING PROTEINS

Muscle meat provides protein, and an array of vitamins, minerals, and amino acids. All meat contains Taurine, with dark poultry meat being one of the best sources. Meat has a very high mineral content and includes essentials like magnesium, zinc, and iron. Meat is a particularly good source of vitamin E and B including B2, B6, and B12. Since you won't be cooking the meat under extreme commercial conditions, the nutrients will gently be retained.

When it comes to choosing the protein, I personally prefer to use a whole animal whenever possible for a few important reasons:

1. Lower in cost

2. More nutrient dense

3. Less wasteful

4. **Creates a delicious and healthy broth - BONUS!** Don't throw out all of the broth, regardless if you use bone-in or boneless meats; it's *packed with nutrients* and is a wonderful addition to the food!

5. Includes skin and fat which creates a healthier and more balanced batch of food

Please note that you'll be deboning the meat and discarding the bones, because cooked bones should never be fed to your pup **(see important safety note on pg. 12)**.

Of course, there are some tradeoffs when using the whole animal, one of which is TIME! It takes longer to process and debone, so go with what works best for you.

A great in-between that is easier to debone and much less time consuming is bone-in chicken thighs (opt for bone-in, skin-on whenever possible). However, I recommend trying to mix things up as much as possible so that there's a good variety of light and dark meats.

Having a good mix of meats also ensures that the different types of fats will be more balanced. For example, try to mix poultry and beef (ruminants, or cud chewing animals) when possible to help balance polyunsaturated and saturated fats. Chicken is higher in polyunsaturated fat and beef is higher in saturated fat, so they help balance each other out.

If you choose to go with deboned meat, just try to use meats that have skin on if possible. In other words, don't always opt for boneless-skinless low calorie, low fat, assuming it will be healthier, because it won't be. Fat is an important ingredient and remember that a lot of it will be rendered down during the cooking process, not to mention there's tons of nutrients in the skin. If you're using ground meats, I recommend up to 80/20 fat percentage for ground meats. Do not exceed 20% fat.

Puppies ideally should eat leaner meats (10%-15% fat) and should not exceed 20% fat. The reason is because there's more phosphorus in lean meats than there is in higher fat meats, and puppies need more phosphorus than adults. Based on lab results for an 80/20 puppy batch I tested, the calcium:phosphorus ratio returned at 2:1. AAFCO minimum is 1:1, and maximum is 2:1. So, you're totally fine to go with 80/20, but a leaner meat option would get you closer to a 1:1 ratio. Exceptions to this would be large breed puppies, discussed on page 38.

If you have a dog that is sensitive to, or has a hard time digesting fat, you can pull the skin and fat off of the meats very easily after cooking during the deboning process at the end, and discard the skin and fat. If your pup is very fat sensitive, or is a breed that is prone to pancreatitis, I recommend going with skinless meats, skinning and defatting the meats yourself prior to cooking, or going with 10%-15% maximum fat content ground meats.

If you have a dog that has pancreatitis, this is a different situation altogether - fat should be avoided at all costs, and you should consult your vet before proceeding with any homemade food.

Great protein options to consider:

- Whole Chicken

- Whole Duck

- Whole Turkey

- Chicken Thighs (with skin and bone is preferred)

- Chicken Breast (with skin and bone is preferred)

- Beef/Bison/Pork/Lamb Roast

- Ground Turkey

- Ground Beef

- Ground Bison

- Ground Lamb

- Kangaroo

- Goat

- Ostrich

- Emu

You may notice that I did not list venison. The reason is because Cervids can be infected with Chronic Wasting Disease, also known as Deer Zombie Disease, and it's something I never risk with my pups or my client's pups. However, there are many dog owners who feed venison (or other Cervids) without any problems. So use your own best judgement, and do what works for you if venison is an ingredient you want or need to use.

VEGGIES

CHOOSING VEGGIES

When choosing the veggies there are some good go-to veggies that are safe, and I have found that dogs love. For purposes of preparation and nutrient preservation, I've listed how some veggies should be prepared (discussed later in the guide in the cooking section). I usually pick two or three veggies for each batch to offer variety, flavor, and nutrients.

For any veggie that is going into the cooker with the rest of the ingredients, use the recommended weight pre-cooked. For any raw veggie that gets added at the end, use the recommended weight as raw.

Get creative but keep in mind that some veggies are not safe for your pup, so you'll always want to make sure you check before adding them to your recipe. You can visit aspca.org/pet-care to check for any ingredient safety.

IMPORTANT SAFETY NOTE Onions are highly toxic to dogs and should never be used as a veggie or a seasoning.

Some veggies you might want to consider:

- **Cooked** (frozen veggies save tons of time):

    - Carrots (can be chopped or put in the pot whole and broken down during the end mixing process)

    - Peas

    - Green Beans

    - Broccoli (roughly chopped - blanched is best)

- **Raw**:

    - Spinach* (blanched or roughly chopped)

    - Cucumber (chopped)

    - Asparagus (blanched or chopped)

    - Zucchini (blanched or finely diced/shredded)

    - Tomatoes (diced raw or canned - just make sure they're fully ripe tomatoes, and never include unripened green tomatoes or any part of the plant's leaves or stems because these contain a toxic glycoalkaloid called solanine)

NUTRITIONAL TIP *If you really want to preserve the nutrients in the veggies, you can put the veggies in a food processor completely raw with a little bit of the cooking broth and puree them. Then just add the veggie puree in at the very end when you're mixing everything together. Or, consider blanching the veggies in the hot cooking liquid at the end for 30-60 minutes instead of fully cooking them if you don't want to puree them. Blanched veggies might not be the best option for picky eaters because they'll be able to easily eat around them.*

*Note that spinach contains oxalates and is not recommended for dogs that have kidney problems.

CARBOHYDRATES

CHOOSING CARBOHYDRATES

Carbohydrates come in many different forms. If you want to stay away from grains, don't choose a carb that is a grain such as rice, oats, or other grain. However, if you choose to go grain free, you may want to provide your dog a supplement that contains taurine. Always use supplements that are made specifically for dogs, and in this case, I would simply search on Amazon, Chewy, or other pet supply retail outlet, for "taurine supplement for dogs", and you should find many available options to choose from. There are growing concerns about Dilated Cardiomyopathy, a sometimes fatal heart condition also known as DCM, in dogs who eat grain free diets. Since there's not a ton of research supported information surrounding the subject, how it can affect some dog breeds differently, and the unknown of whether or not some vegetable fibers can actually bind to taurine and deplete the taurine levels in some dogs, I think it's better to err on the side of caution by adding the additional supplementation until more can be learned.

Adding carbohydrates to the batch offers the opportunity to pack in even more nutrients. All carbohydrates should be cooked to allow for maximum absorption of the nutrients.

For any carb that is going into the cooker with the rest of the ingredients, use the recommended weight pre-cooked. For any carb that gets added at the end, use the recommended weight post-cooked.

Great carb options to consider:

- Sweet Potato (can be chopped or put in the pot whole and broken down during the end mixing process)

- Butternut Squash (peeled, seeded, chopped, and cooked with the batch)

- Potato (can be chopped or put in the pot whole and broken down during the end mixing process)

- Quinoa (cooked and cooled separately and added to the batch at the end)

- Brown Rice (cooked and cooled separately and added to the batch at the end)

- White Rice (easier to digest than brown; cooked and cooled separately and added to the batch at the end)

- Oats (cooked and cooled separately and added to the batch at the end)

- Canned Pumpkin is a super easy option (added at the end)

HELPFUL TIP 1-2 cups of uncooked rice yields about 1 pound cooked. I always cook extra rice and freeze it in a ziplock bag for later so I have pre-cooked rice on-hand (defrost in fridge the night before). Oatmeal is very easy: right before adding to the food, just add ½ pound of oats to a bowl on a scale, and pour in some of the cooking broth (or hot water if you made food on the stovetop instead of using a slow cooker) until you reach 1 pound on the scale (50/50 oats to liquid in weight). Use a broth fat separator if you have one, or try to skim the fat off the top of the broth before adding to the oats. Mix and knead well with your hands until the oats are milky and tender, and all the liquid is absorbed. Add immediately to the food and mix well so the oats don't clump together.*

ORGAN MEATS

CHOOSING ORGAN MEAT

Organ meat is one of the most nutrient dense animal-based foods you'll find anywhere. If you've ever watched a wildlife film, it's no wonder that when a predator takes down the prey, the first thing they go for is the liver, kidneys, and other organs while saving the muscles for last.

Compared to the muscle meat, organ meats are more densely packed with just about every nutrient, including heavy doses of B vitamins such as: B1, B2, B6, folate and the very important vitamin B12. Organ meats are also loaded with minerals like phosphorus, iron, copper, magnesium, iodine, calcium, potassium, sodium, selenium, zinc and manganese and provide the important fat-soluble vitamins A, D, E and K. Organ meats also contain high amounts of essential fatty acids, including arachidonic acid and the omega-3 fats EPA and DHA.

Organ meats are what we will refer to as the vitamins of the batch. It's because of these nutrient rich ingredients that we won't need to add any vitamins in supplement form.

When choosing the organ meat, don't get overwhelmed. Variety is beneficial, so if something is available now and not available later, just go for what's available.

Great organ options to consider (from any animal source - with the exception of some rare / exotic organs that can be too high in some vitamins and should always be checked for safety):

- Liver

- Kidney

- Heart

- Lung

- Spleen

NOTE If possible, always try to incorporate liver: 5%-10% (½ pound - 1 pound) per batch - don't exceed 10% liver. You can use a combination of organ meats up to 15% (1½ pounds) per batch, but do not exceed 15%. I recommend starting at 5%, and gradually increase up to 15% organ combo to avoid tummy upset if your pup isn't used to getting fresh organs. There's very likely enough calcium calculated for added calories and phosphorus from extra organ meat; however, if you decide to add extra organs, it won't hurt to add one extra dose of calcium per pound of extra organs (half dose for a half pound).

NUTRITIONAL TIP For increased vitamin and mineral retention, try blanching the liver &/or other organs by adding to the cooking liquid at the very end, 30-60 minutes before processing, and cook until rare - medium rare. For best results, make sure organs are defrosted/not frozen before blanching. Then when adding to the rest of the food, use a pair of kitchen scissors to easily cut into bite sized chunks. You can also add organs raw to really increase nutrient content (if you're comfortable with that). Reduce freshness storage time to 3-4 days instead of 4-5 (as instructed on page 60) for organs that are raw or cooked rare, and 4-5 days is fine for medium rare.

FRUITS

CHOOSING FRUIT

Adding fruit is like adding even more vitamins, but it also adds fiber which is important for your pup's digestive system. Fiber helps keep the gut healthy, and also aids in expressing the anal glands when your pup takes a poop.

Feel free to get creative here too and include one or a combo of fruits.

IMPORTANT SAFETY NOTE Grapes are highly toxic to dogs and should never be used as a fruit in their food. Raisins are dried grapes, so no raisins either.

Great fruit options:

- Blueberries

- Strawberries (tops/stems removed, whole or chopped)

- Raspberries

- Blackberries

- Bananas (peeled and chopped)

- Apples (chopped - be sure to remove the seeds because they are toxic to dogs)

- Peaches (pitted and chopped - do not give your dogs the pit, leaves, or stem because they are toxic to dogs)

NOTE *Fruit gets added raw at the end and is not cooked.* **Using frozen fruit is a great time saver and helps speed the cooling process.**

TIP *If you have a picky eater who eats around fruits, you might want to consider pureeing them in a blender or food processor before mixing them in with the rest of the food. Just add a little of the cooking broth and blend them up. Your pup won't be able to eat around them this way. Bananas are much harder to eat around since they disintegrate into the food much better, so these are also a great option for picky eaters.*

ESSENTIAL FATTY ACIDS

CHOOSING
ESSENTIAL FATTY ACIDS (EFA's)

When choosing the Essential Fatty Acids, I like to stick to whole foods rather than fish oil. Fish oil can easily go rancid, usually comes from predatory fish which amplifies any toxins as they're passed up the food chain, and many manufacturers supplement the oil with added vitamins, which can quickly reach toxic levels for your furbaby if ingested. For those reasons I stay away.

Alpha-Linolenic Acid: Omega-3
Linoleic Acid: Omega-6

Choosing an EFA is also dependent on the type of meat you choose since we're trying to achieve a good balance of fats: linoleic acid and alpha-linolenic acid (LA and ALA). Fish is a great source because it works with both poultry and beef (ruminants/cud chewing animals), and it adds important EPA and DHA. Fish also adds vitamin D and iodine.

However, to ensure you're including the proper balance of fats for the proper meats, follow these guidelines:

Poultry Recipes (high in LA):
Flaxseed or Chia Seed is higher in ALA, balances the LA:
- Ground Flaxseed or Ground Chia Seed: ¼ cup (great combined with fish)
- Flaxseed or Chia Seed Oil: 3 tablespoons (should be used with lean meats, up to 15% fat - do not combine with fish)

Beef (Ruminant) Recipes (higher in ALA):
Hempseed is higher in LA, balances the ALA:
- Ground Hempseed: ¼ cup (great combined with fish)
- Hempseed Oil: 3 tablespoons (should be used with lean meats, up to 15% fat - do not combine with fish)

Mixed Proteins:
- Choose the protein that weighs the most in the batch

Beef has more ALA than LA, but it doesn't meet the minimum requirements for LA and ALA. If you go with an all beef (ruminant/cud chewing animal) batch of food, ground hempseed or hempseed oil should always be added to ensure there is a good LA and ALA ratio, since hempseed offers an ideal ratio of Omega-6 to Omega-3 for beef.

You can usually find ground flaxseed very easily. However, finding ground chia seed or ground hempseed may be more difficult. In this case, just get chia seeds or raw shelled hempseed, and grind the seeds yourself using a clean coffee grinder, blender, or food processor. The goal here is easier digestion and better absorption for your pup since the whole seeds won't get digested and absorbed.

If you opt for fish as a source of EFA, a good rule of thumb is 1oz of fish per pound of meat. This will ensure a good balance of fats. Also, you don't want to add too much because fish has blood thinning properties. The official rule from AAFCO, *for cats,* is that fish must not exceed 25% of the finished food weight (otherwise vitamin K must be added to assist in blood clotting factors). I realize this isn't a cat food book (and this food shouldn't be fed to cats since formulations for cats is different), but it's a rule I choose to apply for dogs too, just to be safe (you can make your own decision here). You can base your fish weight on the cooked meat weight, or to make it easy, you can base it on the pre-cooked meat weight since neither would exceed 25% of the finished food weight.

Canned fish is such an easy option, and canned sardines are one of my favorites. Just make sure that the can of sardines doesn't have any added flavors. You don't want spicy mustard sardines in your pup's food. Look for sardines packed in olive oil or water, and salt is fine. Don't use sardines packed in other oils, such as corn, soybean, safflower, or sunflower oils that are high in LA - Omega-6.

Some great whole food sources of EFA's include:

- Trout (whole/bone-in is ok)

- Sardines (whole/bone-in is ok)

- Anchovies (whole/bone-in is ok)

- Mackerel (whole/bone-in is ok)

- Salmon (boneless unless canned with bones)

- Tuna (boneless unless canned with bones)

- Herring (whole/bone-in is ok)

- Ground Flaxseed or Cold Pressed Flaxseed Oil

- Ground Chia Seeds or Cold Pressed Chia Seed Oil

- Ground Hempseed or Cold Pressed Hempseed Oil

NOTE Depending on where you live and the type of stores you have available, many of the fish on the list can be purchased raw/whole which is always the best choice. Asian markets are a great resource for raw/whole fish. However, you can also find many of them canned which can make things easy - just make sure the fish is packed in dog-safe ingredients. If you opt for a canned fish, this gets added at the end during the mixing process, and does not get put in the cooker.

IMPORTANT SAFETY NOTE Make sure the plant based EFA you choose doesn't have any harmful supplements. You'll often times find that oils have been fortified with Vitamin D which can be very toxic if the dose isn't just right, so be sure you choose a source that is not fortified in any way.

CALCIUM

CHOOSING/WEIGHING CALCIUM

When determining how much calcium to use, you'll want to familiarize yourself with the nutritional label of the calcium you choose; this will help you to determine how much calcium you'll need. Every bottle could be different, so it's important to look at the calcium content per serving.

Powdered calcium will need to be given at 1250-3000 mg per pound of food (3000 mg for puppies up to 1 year of age: *see important note on pg. 38*), with a maximum of 4500 mg for large breeds, and 6250 mg for small and medium breeds (though this amount should only ever be used as a buffer and you should never try to reach the maximums). This means that you'll need to know the amount of calcium mg's per serving for your particular bottle of calcium, and translate that serving into an amount that equals 1250 mg of calcium for adults, and 3000 mg for puppies. The easiest and most accurate way to do this is by weight in grams (g), so you'll want to determine how much calcium is in a serving by weight.

For example, let's say that the calcium bottle reads that one serving equals 800 mg of calcium, and that serving weighs 2.8 g. You'll want to calculate like this for adult dogs:

- 1250 divided by 800 = 1.56
- 1.56 x 2.8 g = 4.38 g
- Calcium = 4.38 g by weight per pound of food
(Example: 10 pounds of food: 10 x 4.38 g = 43.8 g of calcium)

So, for this example, you would need 4.38 g of calcium by weight in order to equal 1250 mg of calcium. But remember, we have a range of 1250-3000 mg, so you could round up to 4.5 g of calcium by weight, per pound of food, and be just fine. ***Easier:** You can also use the same calculation to determine servings based on measurements (teaspoon) instead of weight to keep things super easy. For example, if a serving is 1 tsp, and that serving is 800 mg, 1250 divided by 800 = 1.56 tsp; so for this example, just use 1.5 teaspoons per pound of food and call it good.

KEEP THINGS EASY TIP* Since the sample recipes average approx. 8000 calories and 10 pounds, you can base your calcium calculation on a final batch weight of 10 pounds without the hassle of weighing all of the food at the end (with the exception of the note for puppies on page 38**). Because the calcium calculation is enough to cover some excess food weight based on calories, you're fine to be over weight by a pound or two (even more if extra organs &/or eggs were added).* ***However, you may want to weigh your first few batches just to make sure you're getting close, and adjust accordingly.***

It's important to have a scale that can weigh in grams and tenths of grams. I have a separate gram scale just for weighing my calcium. The reason is, it's nice to know if you're at 4.5 grams, for example, rather than have a scale that jumps from 4 to 5 grams. *NOTE* Depending on your scale and calcium weight needed, keep it easy and just round up or down to the closest weight increment in grams. Once you've determined how much calcium you'll need for each pound of finished food, it's very helpful to write that amount on the calcium bottle so that you can easily refer back to it later without having to come to this page every time. **Refer to page 38 for calcium calculation adjustments based on meat fat percentages**.

Eggshells are a natural form of calcium carbonate and make a very easy option - just be sure to wash them with warm water before grinding them in case they were sprayed with any chemicals from the producer. Eggshells can easily be ground up in your hand using your fingers, using a clean coffee grinder, blender, or food processor, or put them into a plastic bag and smash them using a rolling pin. They don't have to be completely powdered, so don't worry if there are some bits and chunks – your dog will be able to consume them just fine. They should ideally be used with leaner meats, up to 10% fat, to ensure there's enough phosphorus to balance the calcium (higher fat meats contain less phosphorus). Eggshell powder can also be used. Eggshells contain approx. 1140 mg of calcium per 3g shell, and eggshell powder is approx. 1900 mg per tsp (check the label to confirm calcium content). So keep things easy, and use 1 ground shell or 1 tsp eggshell powder per pound of food, or follow the package instructions if your eggshell powder is for pets - easiest option.

***NOTE* Eggshells, calcium carbonate, and calcium citrate do not provide phosphorus and should only be used with lean meats (refer to calcium and meat guide on page 39). Bone meal adds the perfect ratio of calcium and phosphorus making it much easier to balance, can be paired with any meat fat percentage, and is the only form of calcium that should be used for growing puppies and pregnant/nursing dogs.**

If this is overwhelming, get Better Bones dried bone meal that can be found at thenaturaldogstore.com and follow the package instructions, or refer to their website for guidance based on the meat fat percentage you used.

***NOTE* Calcium amounts are based on 1000 kcal (1000 Calories) per pound of food (1.25 mg - 3 mg of calcium per Calorie). To be sure you stay within a safe threshold while maintaining a good calcium to phosphorus balance, refer to the note on page 38.**

(Photo shown using raw meat instead of cooked meat)

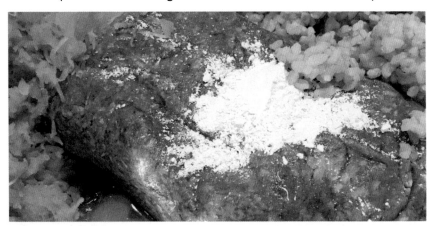

IMPORTANT NOTE Adjusting calcium based on Calories is important since calcium is calculated on a caloric basis (1.25 mg - 3 mg of calcium per Calorie). For leaner meats **(10%-15% fat)**, base the calcium calculation (pg. 36) at 1800 mg per pound of food for puppies and adults sharing puppy food. This means that a 10 pound batch of food would get 18,000 mg of calcium per batch instead of 30,000 mg. Basing final batch weight at 6 pounds using standard calcium amounts will result in the same calculation - this is the method I personally use because it's easier for me to remember adjusted final batch weights, rather than adjusted calcium amounts, but again, they both deliver the same number. **No adjustment needed for adults.**

This is not recommended unless you increase feeding amounts to ensure your dog gets enough Calories per day: If you go with all boneless, skinless white meat, such as turkey or chicken breast or other extra lean, low calorie meat **(1%-5% fat)**, base the calcium calculation (pg. 36) at 1500 mg per pound of food for puppies and adults sharing puppy food. This means that a 10 pound batch of food would get 15,000 mg of calcium per batch instead of 30,000 mg. Basing final batch weight at 5 pounds using standard calcium amounts will result in the same calculation. **No adjustment needed for adults.**

LARGE BREEDS Higher fat meats require more calcium (bone meal) for puppies to ensure they get enough phosphorus. For this reason, large breed puppies that will grow to 70 pounds or more as adults (and any small breed puppies or small/large breed adults sharing their food), should only be fed the lower 10%-15% fat ratio recipes, that in-turn require less calcium. Once adulthood is reached, up to 20% fat is fine.

Some great calcium sources include:

- **Bone Meal - Adults & Puppies:**
  - **Adults:** 1250 mg per pound of food
  - **Puppies & Adults Sharing Puppy Food:** 3000 mg per pound of food **(with the exception of note on page 38)**
  - #1 preferred, provides proper ratio of calcium and phosphorus for any meat fat percentage, includes extra vitamins and minerals, and is the _only_ *form of calcium that should be used for growth & reproduction*

- **Ground Eggshells or Eggshell Powder - Adults Only:** If using whole eggshells, don't waste the eggs - mix up to 10 whole eggs per batch in at the end, and let the heat from the food gently cook them, or you could boil them, and crumble them up before adding to the food

    - 1 washed and ground eggshell per pound of food

    - 1 teaspoon eggshell powder per pound of food, or follow package instructions if you have eggshell powder for pets - easiest option

- **Calcium Carbonate - Adults Only:** 1250 mg per pound of food

- **Calcium Citrate - Adults Only:** 1250 mg per pound of food, and is *the only form of calcium on this page that should be used for dogs with history of kidney stones, or as instructed by your veterinarian*

Calcium and Meat Guide:
- 20% fat: Bone Meal
- 15% fat: Bone Meal
- 10% fat: Bone Meal, Egg Shells, Calcium Carbonate/Citrate
- 05% fat: Bone Meal, Egg Shells, Calcium Carbonate/Citrate
- 01% fat: Bone Meal, Egg Shells, Calcium Carbonate/Citrate

Be sure to refer to page 38 for information on different meat fat percentages in relation to calcium calculations for puppies.

IMPORTANT SAFETY NOTE Check the label on any powdered calcium source to make sure there aren't any harmful added ingredients, and **use food-grade only**. If your dog has a history of stones or has kidney problems that requires a reduced phosphorus/ higher fat diet, bone meal should never be used, and food should not be made without further guidance from your veterinarian or veterinary nutritionist. **Never give your dog cooked bones (see note on pg. 12).**

ASSEMBLY

Putting it all Together – Makes Approximately 10 Pounds of Food

Now it's time to finally get started and make your dog's food. I'll split the recipes up into two different categories to make things easy:

1. Using Bone-In Meat

2. Using Boneless Meat

Don't forget the broth!

Once you're done with the food, don't forget that yummy broth (in either recipe version) because it makes a great addition to the food. I can't stress enough just how nutritious it is for your pup. It's packed with all kinds of vitamins, minerals, and amino acids, and it's completely free! So fill up some containers instead of throwing it all out, and add a couple spoonfuls to your pup's food. *Just be sure to remove the fat cap before serving.* Broth will stay good in the fridge for 6-8 days, and in the freezer for many months if stored in a freezer safe container.

Don't forget to HAVE FUN! This should never be stressful. Keep in mind how in-tuned our dogs are and any stress you emit will come through to them, and in the food.

Just be patient with yourself and try to realize that as with anything in life, practice and persistence will soon make the process much easier. And don't forget to give yourself a good pat on the back because you're doing something absolutely WONDERFUL that will shine through in your pup's health and happiness!

Another thing I want to mention is that the variations are limitless. *Variety is the key to ensure nutrients aren't being missed.* Think of the main recipe as the foundation, and create variety by swapping ingredients for others. For example, go with blueberries one time, and maybe banana the next. Just be sure that you stick within the food groups, and follow the weights and measurements for the recipe foundation to ensure everything is balanced.

You can also add different whole food supplements to create an even more nutrient rich meal. As a matter of fact, I have a whole menu dedicated to just that, called the 'Add-Ons' menu. Just be sure to check that an ingredient is safe for your pup before you add it to their food. A great resource for this is aspca.org/pet-care.

Below are some great supplements you might want to consider adding. These can be added to the batch or to individual servings:

1. Nonfat Unsweetened Greek Yogurt (never get yogurt that is "sugar free"; instead, always go for "unsweetened" so you don't risk some kind of artificial sweetener). Great source of probiotics. Add a small spoonful to each meal.

2. Eggs are a great source of vitamin D, are packed with all kinds of nutrients, and I highly recommend using them if your pup can have them - 10 total per batch (total includes any used in conjunction with egg shells for calcium).

3. Fish (add fish to the batch only if using a non-oil plant based EFA at 1 ounce of fish maximum per pound of cooked or pre-cooked meat weight - refer to page 32-34 for more info).

Start sparingly with the ones below to make sure your pup likes it:

4. Wheat Grass Powder (1 Tbsp per batch – or just a pinch to individual meals).

5. *Turmeric (1-3 tsp per batch – or just a pinch to individual meals).

6. *Spirulina (1 tsp per batch – or just a pinch to individual meals).

*Make sure you get these from a reliable and safe source that tests for contaminants.

SAMPLE RECIPES

Recipe Example #1
Using Bone-In Meat
Yields: Approximately 10-11 Pounds

Ingredients:

•9 pounds meat (a little more weight than the boneless meat recipe to make up for lost weight in discarded bone):

•6½ - 7 pounds whole &/or bone-in, skin-on chicken combo – frozen or thawed

•2 pounds 80/20 ground beef – frozen or tightly packed thawed

•2 pounds veggies

•Determine if your veggies will be cooked or raw by referring to page 19

•1 pound carbohydrates

•Determine if your carb is cooked separate or if it goes in the cooking pot by referring to page 22

•½ pound (8 ounces) beef liver (you can use up to 1½ pounds organ combo, see page 26 for more info)

•½ pound (8 ounces) fruit

•¼ cup ground flaxseed and 1-2 cans of sardines (up to 8 ounces)

•12,500 mg bone meal for adults, 30,000 mg bone meal for puppies & adults sharing puppy food (Calcium based on 10 pounds of finished food - see exceptions on page 38)

•2 teaspoons salt (I prefer Himalayan) - required for puppies, adults optional

Instructions:

1. If you are using any veggies from the 'Cooked Veggies' list, you'll wash, chop, and place them in the cooker first. If you're using any of the other more delicate veggies from the raw list, they will get put in raw at the end, so save them for later. You can also put some of the more delicate veggies, like broccoli, in the cooker last/on top, so they don't break down as much. To preserve even more nutrients, consider blanching the veggies or pureeing them raw and adding them at the end. See tip on page 19 for more info.

2. Determine what carbs you'll be using, and if you're going with something that gets added to the batch, wash, chop, and place them in the cooker next. If you're using a carb that gets added to the batch later, follow any cooking instructions for that carb (ahead of time or closer to the end of the batches cook time) allow it to fully cool, and add it in at the end - I'll remind you in the upcoming steps.

3. Place the meat containing bones in the cooker – if you used a whole bird, place it in the cooker belly down.

4. Place ground meat in cooker (if you opted for some ground meat). It can squish in together with the bone-in meat (frozen is a great option here).

5. If you opted for raw fish as the EFA, add it now. Just add fish whole, and don't worry about the bones if using bone-in fish because the bones will easily break down during the mixing process at the end. It helps if bone-in fish is submerged when you add the water, but it's not absolutely necessary.

6. Add organ meat. It's ok to have this stacked on top of the other meats (don't worry about submerging them in the water). Just make sure your lid will close. **You can also blanch organs at the end to preserve nutrients (recommended) - see tip on page 26 for more info.**

7. Fill with water (if your meat is frozen, add a little less water so that you don't overflow during the cooking process). I leave about 2-3 inches of head space in my cooker so that it doesn't overflow. Don't worry if the meat isn't completely submerged – it will be fine.

8. Cover cooker with lid and set at 225 degrees Fahrenheit if cooker has a temp setting, or Low if cooker has High/Low setting.

9. Cook for 8-10 hours. I like to put everything in the cooker before I go to bed, and then get up and process it all in the morning – OR – I'll put it on in the morning and process later in the day.

10. Once the meat has cooked for 8-10 hours or has reached an internal temperature of 165 degrees Fahrenheit, turn off the cooker, lift the insert out of the cooker using oven mitts or some other form of protection so you don't burn your hands, and set the insert next to your extra-large "MAIN BOWL". This will be used as your main mixing bowl.

11. Using two heavy duty strong metal spoons (or large spider skimmer if one is available), put one on each side of the whole chicken (if a whole bird was used) and lift the chicken out of the cooking liquid, and place into your main bowl. **Debone and discard the bones as you go (never give your dog cooked bones - see important safety note on pg. 12).** I find that it's much easier to debone one scoop at a time because it helps keep track of the bones as you go. Continue this process with the rest of the meat.

12. Scoop out the remaining ingredients from the cooking liquid into the main bowl.

13. Mix everything together by breaking up the meats and mixing with the other ingredients. You'll want to break up any clumps of organ meat. If you blanched your organs, kitchen scissors work really well to cut them up. **Be sure to pay special attention to any chunks of fish that may need to be broken down by really crumbling the fish and bones** (if you opted for any raw bone-in fish). You can also put the fish in a blender with some broth if you really want to make it easy - just puree the fish and bone, and pour it in with the rest of the food.

14. **You'll also want to go through everything really well to make sure you didn't miss any bones that need to be discarded from the bone-in meats.** I find it easiest to do this by hand so it's easier to feel for any bones.

15. Add your fruit. It's helpful if using frozen fruit so that it can help cool things down.

16. If you opted for any raw veggies, add them now.

17. If you opted for a plant based or canned fish EFA, add it now.

18. If you went with a carb that gets added at the end, add it now.

19. Add 2 teaspoons of salt (required for puppies, optional for adults).

20. You can skip to step 21 and base your calcium calculation on 10 pounds of finished food (with the exception of note for puppies on page 38). Or, if you prefer to weigh the batch, get your extra-large "WEIGHT BOWL" and place it on your scale. Be sure to zero out the weight of the scale so you aren't calculating the weight of your bowl. Transfer all of the food from your main bowl into the weight bowl on the scale and write down the weight of your food. Writing it down will help ensure you don't forget while calculating your calcium.

21. Calculate the amount of calcium you'll need (see page 36) and add it now. Mixing powdered calcium with a little water is helpful. Add to the batch and stir well to combine.

22. If the food turns out thick, stir in some of the cooking broth. This also adds extra nutrients that were lost to the liquid during the cooking process.

23. **COOL THE FOOD DOWN PRIOR TO PACKAGING** See the 'Cooling' section of this guide for info on how to safely cool the food.

24. Divide into storage containers or freezer bags and freeze.

25. Don't forget to save some of that nutritious broth! Add a couple spoonfuls to each meal for your pup, and they'll love you for it!

Recipe Example #2
Using Boneless Ground Meat
Yields: Approximately 10-11 Pounds

Ingredients:

- 8 pounds boneless meat:

    - 6 pounds 85/15 ground turkey – frozen or tightly packed thawed

    - 2 pounds 85/15 ground beef – frozen or tightly packed thawed

- 2 pounds veggies

    - Determine if your veggies will be cooked or raw by referring to page 19

- 1 pound carbohydrates

    - Determine if your carb is cooked separate or if it goes in the cooking pot by referring to page 22

- ½ pound (8 ounces) beef liver (you can use up to 1½ pounds organ combo, see page 26 for more info)

- ½ pound (8 ounces) fruit

- ¼ cup ground flaxseed and 1-2 cans of sardines (up to 8 ounces)

- 12,500 mg bone meal for adults, 18,000 mg bone meal for puppies & adults sharing puppy food (Calcium based on 10 pounds of finished food for adults, and 6 pounds of finished food for puppies - see exceptions on page 38)

- 2 teaspoons salt (I prefer Himalayan) - required for puppies, adults optional

Instructions:

1. If you are using any veggies from the 'Cooked Veggies' list, you'll wash, chop, and place them in the cooker first. If you're using any of the other more delicate veggies from the raw list, they will get put in raw at the end so save them for later. You can also put some of the more delicate veggies, like broccoli, in the cooker last/on top, so they don't break down as much. To preserve even more nutrients, consider blanching the veggies or pureeing them raw and adding them at the end. See tip on page 19 for more info.

2. Determine what carbs you'll be using, and if you're going with something that gets added to the batch, wash, chop, and place them in the cooker next. If you're using a carb that gets added to the batch later, follow any cooking instructions for that carb (ahead of time or closer to the end of the batches cook time) allow it to fully cool, and add it in at the end - I'll remind you in the upcoming steps.

3. Place meat in cooker.

4. If you opted for raw fish as the EFA, add it now. Just add fish whole, and don't worry about the bones if using bone-in fish because the bones will easily break down during the mixing process at the end. It helps if bone-in fish is submerged when you add the water, but it's not absolutely necessary.

5. Add organ meat. It's ok to have this stacked on top of the other meats (don't worry about submerging them in the water). Just make sure your lid will close. **You can also blanch organs at the end to preserve nutrients (recommended) - see tip on page 26 for more info.**

6. Fill with water (if your meat is frozen, add a little less water so that you don't overflow during the cooking process). I leave about 2-3 inches of head space in my cooker so that it doesn't overflow. Don't worry if the meat isn't completely submerged – it will be fine.

7. Cover cooker with lid and set at 225 degrees Fahrenheit if cooker has a temp setting, or Low if cooker has High/Low setting.

8. Cook for 8-10 hours. I like to put everything in the cooker before I go to bed, and then get up and process it all in the morning – OR – I'll put it on in the morning and process later in the day.

9. Once the meat has cooked for 8-10 hours or has reached an internal temperature of 165 degrees Fahrenheit, turn off the cooker, lift the insert out of the cooker using oven mitts or some other form of protection so you don't burn your hands, and set the insert next to your extra-large "MAIN BOWL". This will be used as your main mixing bowl.

10. Scoop out the ingredients from the cooking liquid into the main bowl.

11. Mix everything together by breaking up the meats and mixing with the other ingredients. You'll want to break up any clumps of organ meat. If you blanched your organs, kitchen scissors work really well to cut them up. **Be sure to pay special attention to any chunks of fish that may need to be broken down by really crumbling the fish and bones** (if you opted for any raw bone-in fish). I find it easiest to do this by hand so it's easier to feel for any bones. You can also put the fish in a blender with some broth if you really want to make it easy - just puree the fish and bone, and pour it in with the rest of the food.

12. Add your fruit. It's helpful if using frozen fruit so that it can help cool things down.

13. If you opted for any raw veggies, add them now.

14. If you opted for a plant based or canned fish EFA, add it now.

15. If you went with a carb that gets added at the end, add it now.

16. Add 2 teaspoons of salt (required for puppies, optional for adults).

17. You can skip to step 18 and base your calcium calculation on 10 pounds of finished food (with the exception of note for puppies on page 38). Or, if you prefer to weigh the batch, get your extra-large "WEIGHT BOWL" and place it on your scale. Be sure to zero out the weight of the scale so you aren't calculating the weight of your bowl. Transfer all of the food from your main bowl into the weight bowl on the scale and write down the weight of your food. Writing it down will help ensure you don't forget while calculating your calcium.

18. Calculate the amount of calcium you'll need (see page 36) and add it now. Mixing powdered calcium with a little water is helpful. Add to the batch and stir well to combine.

19. If the food turns out thick, stir in some of the cooking broth. This also adds extra nutrients.

20. **COOL THE FOOD DOWN PRIOR TO PACKAGING** See the 'Cooling' section of this guide for info on how to safely cool the food.

21. Divide into storage containers or freezer bags and freeze.

22. Don't forget to save some of that nutritious broth! Add a couple spoonfuls to each meal for your pup, and they'll love you for it!

COOLING, STORAGE, & FEEDING

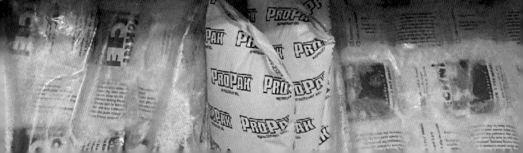

COOLING

Be sure to cool the food down prior to packaging, otherwise you risk bacteria growing in the food. The FDA recommends reaching 70 degrees Fahrenheit (F) within the first 2 hours of cooling, and 41 degrees (F) within the next 4 hours, for a maximum total of 6 hours cooling time. If you can reach 41 degrees (F) sooner, great! The best way to cool food is to divide it into shallow cooling containers so that the food is 2 inches or less in depth, and put the uncovered containers in the fridge, or even better, in the freezer which will allow the food to cool much faster. I always set a 45 minute timer to check the food temp so I don't forget. You can also mix in up to 2 cups of ice (results in a soupier stew style final product, but helps speed the cooling process).

STORAGE

Food and broth must be kept refrigerated or frozen at all times. Treat it just like you would your own food, and don't leave it out for too long. When stored in an airtight container, food will keep in the refrigerator for 4-5 days, and in the freezer for many months. Freezer times will vary depending on the storage vessel used. Broth is good in the fridge for 6-8 days, and in the freezer for many months.

Zip lock baggies work great because you can get a lot of the air out which will aid in longer storage times. Just be sure to use freezer style bags.

I highly recommend writing on the storage containers, a calendar of some type, or a sign on the fridge so you don't lose track of how long it's been in the fridge. The last thing you want to do is feed your dog food that has gone bad!

It's also safe to freeze, defrost, and immediately re-freeze if needed. Just make sure the defrost time is short and does not exceed the freshness "good until" date. In other words, if it's been sitting in the fridge fully defrosted for 3 days, it's ready to expire and shouldn't be re-frozen.

PREPARATION & THAWING

From frozen, it will really depend on the storage vessel used. The smaller the vessel, the shorter the thawing time. Defrost in the refrigerator, or you could certainly defrost in the microwave using your defrost setting and following your microwave's defrost instructions. Just be sure you're using microwave safe storage vessels.

From fresh, there is no need to thaw. However, if you have dogs that don't like cold food, I recommend warming up some of the broth in the microwave or on the stovetop and mixing it with the food, or warm up the food by adding some hot water and stirring it up. This will bring the food to a more room-temperature state.

FEEDING

The methods I teach you here are so much easier and less confusing than trying to calculate caloric content. It's how I've been feeding my dogs, and instructing my clients to feed their dogs, successfully for years.

Dogs 12 Months & Older: 2%-4% of your dog's body weight per day divided into two meals daily. Depending on the caloric content of the batch of food, and your dog's activity levels and metabolism, you may need to increase or decrease accordingly. 3% is a good starting point for most adult dogs.

Feeding Puppies: These portions are a good guide. Make sure to maintain a healthy weight that supports your pup's growth, and increase serving sizes if needed based on your pup's rate of growth, activity levels, and metabolism.

•8 - 12 Months: 4%-3% of your puppy's body weight per day, split into two meals

•6 - 8 Months: 6%-4% of your puppy's body weight per day, split into two meals

•4 - 6 Months: 8%-6% of your puppy's body weight per day, split into three meals

•2 - 4 Months: 10%-8% of your puppy's body weight per day, split into three meals

•OR 2%-4% of your puppy's expected adult body weight per day, split into two or three meals

TIP *Make sure to maintain a healthy weight. Always base the feeding portions on your dog's preferred weight. If your dog is overweight, feed based on the preferred healthy weight that your dog should be. If your dog is underweight, again, feed portions based on the preferred healthy weight that your dog should be. Always make sure you keep food bowls clean, and that your pup has access to fresh, clean drinking water at all times.*

To figure this out, you'll need to know how much your dog/ puppy weighs. An easy way to do this is to step on a scale and weigh yourself, and then weigh yourself again while holding your pup. Subtract the weight of you from the combined weight of you and your dog, and this will tell you how much your dog weighs.

Feeding Example: Dog weighs 15 pounds. Using a calculator: 15 x 3% = 0.45 pounds. Now take 0.45 x 16 and this will give you the daily amount in ounces which would equal 7.2 ounces per day split into two meals (3.6 ounces, or just round up to 4 ounces per meal). You don't need to convert to ounces if your calculation ends in a pound or more. Converting to ounces just makes it easier for smaller portions. It's easier to weigh 3.6 ounces than it is to weigh 0.23 pounds (as an example).

Transitioning: It's always a good idea to transition from your pup's old food to the new food slowly. I recommend mixing in 1/4 new food with 3/4 old food on the first day, 1/2 and 1/2 on the second day, 3/4 new to 1/4 old on the 3rd day, and by the fourth day eliminating the old food altogether. Poop is a key determining factor in the transition process. If your pup has a bout of runnier poop, slow the transition. **Just be sure that the food is kept fresh and doesn't expire during this time.** Food can safely be defrosted and immediately refrozen if you think you'll need smaller amounts in the fridge to make sure and keep things fresh during the transition. Once your dog has transitioned to the new fresh food that you're making, transitioning between different recipes is not typically necessary. However, be your pup's best judge.

Calories will fluctuate based on the ingredients you choose. For example, oatmeal is higher in Calories than rice or pumpkin. Higher fat meats also contain more Calories. Typically, recipes will range from 400-700 kcal/pound (figure is approximate).

64

RESOURCES
FOR PRODUCTS I USE

I found almost every item I use (including calcium supplements) on Amazon.com. I would include links here, but since the sellers aren't always a sure thing for inventory, I feel that it would be better suited to provide you with item details and then you can search for the best deal on your own.

- •Oster 22-quart roaster oven (by far my favorite and worth every penny) - any 22-quart cooker will do fine (you can do 2 batches in these cookers - just make sure you have an oversized mixing tub, and enough fridge/freezer space to cool down and store all that food)

- •Crock Pot 7-quart cooker

- •Accuteck 86 Lbs Digital Scale

- •0.01oz/0.1g 3000g Digital Gram Scale

- •Spider Skimmer (large strainer ladle is great for pulling ingredients, including whole birds, out of the cooker)

- •Catering Pans (2 inch, 4 inch, 6 inch depth) make great mixing/cooling pans, and can be purchased on Amazon or at any restaurant supply store

- •LEM Meat Lug - makes a great oversized mixing tub

- •Better Bones Bone Meal (thenaturaldogstore.com)

- •NOW Foods Bone Meal

- •Nutricost or NOW Foods Calcium Citrate

- •Nutricost or NOW Foods Calcium Carbonate

- •Amazing Grass Organic Wheat Grass Powder

- •ZHOU Spirulina Powder

ABOUT THE AUTHOR

Angela Gertino

Angela Gertino is a dog lover to her core. She has spent many years creating food for her furry family, which was stemmed from her sweet boy, Chance, who was diagnosed with Congestive Heart Failure (CHF). Once Chance was diagnosed, she made it her mission to make sure he was eating the best food possible. She started researching healthy, fresh food diets for dogs, and the incredible role diet can play for prolonged life for a dog that has been diagnosed with CHF. It was in 2013 when she committed to making fresh homemade food for her pets, and she never looked back. Chance survived for two full years with CHF, until his little heart just couldn't go anymore.

She continued to make food for all of her furry companions, until one day she saw a documentary about the pet food industry called *Pet Fooled*. After watching that movie, her life was changed forever. It was the very next day that she set out to build and open a business that creates healthy food for pets, and that is when Mindful Mutt LLC was born. She has been a successful pet food manufacturer and business owner since 2017.

She later studied and expanded her education, and is now a Certified Raw Dog Food Nutrition Specialist, and Certified Pet Food Nutrition Specialist. It is her goal to make sure that pet parents everywhere have the tools available to provide their furry companions with the most nutritious and healthy food they possibly can, at a price they can afford, so that their furbabies can live long, happy, and healthy lives.

For the love of dogs everywhere.

Made in the USA
Monee, IL
21 May 2022

96672367R00048